The Art of
Boxing

The Complete Guide to Boxing Training

Jim Burns

JA-Tech Studios Limited

The Art of Boxing

Copyright © JA-Tech Studios Limited.

All rights reserved. The right of Jim Burns to be identified as the author of this work has been asserted in accordance with the Copyright, Designs and Patents Act of 1988.

No part of this book may be reproduced by any means, nor translated into a machine language, without the written permission of the publisher.

JA-Tech Studios Ltd
Publications Department
178a Grange Road
Longford
Coventry
West Midlands
CV6 6DA
United Kingdom

Photographs by David W Monks
Member of the Master Photographer's Association
Snappy Snaps Portrait Studio
7 Cross Cheaping
Coventry
CV1 1HF

Cover Artwork by David Penfound - Artwork International

A CIP Catalogue for this book is available from the British Library.

Printed and bound in Great Britain by Redwood Books, Wiltshire

ISBN 0 9536997 0 6

Acknowledgements

Although the art of Boxing only took a few months to write it was 25 years in the making. In those 25 years I have met some wonderful and interesting people. I would like to specially thank a few of those people, for without their help, I would not be here today.

To my friend and mentor Geoff Thompson. Thank you Geoff for showing me the light.

To my two daughters Andrea and Josephine. Thank you for your love and friendship.

To my mum and my family for putting up with me through the dark years. My love to you all.

To my friend and business partner, Al Peasland, for enabling me to look forward to a bright and prosperous future.

To my first coach, Eric Crow, for teaching me the importance of good technique and thorough preparation.

A special mention to all of my coaches and training partners, especially Bob Spour, Jim McDonell and Bob Sykes.

Dedication

About three years ago I found myself at a very low point in my life, filled with despair and despondency. I was about to give up and throw in the towel. I didn't know it at the time, but I was about to start on a long journey that would change my life forever. Three years on I am now well into my journey and feel it's time I thanked the person who helped make it all possible.

Although the pieces to the jigsaw were there all along, this person helped me to fit them together. Geoff Thompson showed me that it was possible to change and improve one's life by looking inward to your heart for the answers.

This book brings to an end the first part of my journey and I would like to dedicate it to my friend and mentor Geoff Thompson, without whose help I would still be living in darkness. I would never have had the courage to take the first step. Thank you Geoff.

Contents

	PAGE
FOREWORD	1
ABOUT THE AUTHOR	3
INTRODUCTION	7
CHAPTER ONE EQUIPMENT	9
CHAPTER TWO SAFETY	11
CHAPTER THREE STANCE	15
CHAPTER FOUR BASIC PUNCHES	23
CHAPTER FIVE DEFENCE	31
CHAPTER SIX HOOKS & UPPERCUTS	39
CHAPTER SEVEN COMBINATIONS	49
CHAPTER EIGHT ADVANCED FOOTWORK	61
CHAPTER NINE PARTNER WORK	65
CHAPTER TEN COUNTER ATTACKING	71
CHAPTER ELEVEN FITNESS	79
CHAPTER TWELVE SPARRING	95
CHAPTER THIRTEEN WHY BOXING?	97

Foreword

BY JIM McDONELL

One of only three people ever to have beaten the legendary Barry McGuigan. Once in a while a book comes along that breaks new ground. In writing this book, Jim Burns has opened the door to the secret world of boxing and allowed us to look inside.

The Art of Boxing offers a real insight into what many would say is one of the toughest sports of all. Jim as started right at the beginning and with the help of easy to follow photographs and instructions, takes you right through to advanced combinations and footwork.

As an ex-professional boxer and now a full time professional boxing trainer, I found the book both enjoyable and informative and I am sure you will too. Reading through the book it's easy to see why the Art of Boxing has been so successful. Jim is a genuine fight fan with a real feel for the noble art.

As a professional trainer, I think this is a must for all real fight fans and I am sure you will get as much pleasure and enjoyment from the book as I have.

Jim McDonell - Professional Coach

The Art of Boxing

About the Author

For more than twenty five years Jim Burns has been involved with Boxing both in the Amateur and Professional scene. Jim has spent many years studying the art of boxing and knows that there is more to this noble art than just throwing punches at a moving target.

Jim has also studied other forms of ring craft, including Muay Thai Boxing and, after gaining his 10th Khan qualification, went on to qualify as a Muay Thai Boxing Coach as well as a judge and referee.

To add to his impressive array of qualifications relating to the ring, Jim has also gained a coaching position within the highly respected British Combat Association, the U.K.'s leading self defence association.

The Art of Boxing

Jim has spent many years studying many types of ring craft and, although his qualifications are impressive to say the least, he still regards his highest achievement as gaining his license to coach boxing professionally under the British Boxing Board of Control. An honour that is only given to a privileged few.

The culmination of studying and writing about boxing has resulted in the publication of this book, which covers not only the physics of boxing, but also the psychology of what has to be one of the most intense sports in the world today. Because of his experience and knowledge he is recognised as an expert in his field and has recently been offered the opportunity to write for a national Martial Arts magazine.

Unfortunately, a few uneducated people sometimes consider boxing barbaric. Because of this, Jim has decided to dispel the myths that surround boxing and show for the first time in simple to understand language a real insight into the world of boxing.

Jim hold regular seminars around the country which are attended by a wide selection of people, not only from the boxing and martial arts world, but also people from all walks of life, who often wonder what boxing is all about, but were too frightened to step into a boxing gym. Because Jim's coaching techniques are as varied as the people who come along to watch, the seminars are enjoyable and everyone leaves with a smile as well as a better understanding of what is a wonderful art form.

About The Author

Although boxing is a highly skilled and specialised fighting form, Jim has long held the belief that anyone can gain something from boxing, even if it is just a higher level of fitness and self awareness. Jim fought competitively for eight years but understands fully that not everyone wants to take boxing that far.

The art of boxing is already being haled as a break through in the world of coaching and is set to become a 'classic', not that it will effect Jim. He can still remember the first time he walked into the Edgwick Boxing Club way back in 1969 and to quote the author, "Boxing has been a part of my life for as long as I can remember, and I will continue to coach and talk about this noble art as long as people are interested in what makes boxing the unique art form it is!"

Introduction

Boxing has been with us in one form or another for many hundreds of years. Although the fights we watch on television today bare no resemblance to the deadly battles of years gone by, they are still exciting to watch, making many of us gasp with amazement as the two warriors battle it out, blow for blow.

The fighters of today are highly specialised fighting machines. Comparing a fighter of today with a fighter from sixty or seventy years ago, would be like comparing a Formula One racing car to a Model T Ford.

Very few, if any forms of unarmed combat are as specialised as boxing is. No other fighting art spends as much time and effort on perfecting the warrior for the fight.

Few people can really comprehend the ferocity or the intensity of a fight between two highly skilled opponents. The taste of battle is something that has been left behind in history, at least for most of us. One or two gladiators still recognise the pump of adrenaline, that feeling of danger in your gut, the smell of fear in the air.

The truth is, society has sanitised us to the extent that most of us will never know the feeling of standing on the edge of the unknown, ready to take that final step. The step that few are brave enough to take, content instead to look in from the safety of the outside and wonder what it might be like.

As you work through this book, you will begin to understand the real fight, the physical prowess, the emotional torment, the spoils of battles won. You will start to understand that boxing is not just about hitting him harder than he can hit you, but about being true to yourself, to look into your deepest sole and accept what you find.

Boxing is an excellent way to keep fit as well as learning one of the most effective forms of self defence known to man.

But beyond that, boxing is a way of life. A way of bringing the body and sole together as one. Few people take up the challenge, and even fewer make it through to the other side, but if you do, you will be rewarded with a unique feeling of peace and contentment.

Perhaps you might be thinking I have lost the plot, well you might be right, but believe me when I tell you that boxing is far more than standing toe to toe with another boxer.

If you enjoy boxing as a way of keeping fit, then enjoy and be happy. If, however, you want to go all the way to the top, and are prepared to make the sacrifices then you will not be disappointed in the end result.

CHAPTER ONE
Equipment

The good news about boxing, and more to the point, boxing equipment is that, in the main, there are very few "New" innovations or dynamic new training techniques that will revolutionise your punching power. At least none that I've heard of.

The bad news is that boxing training is recognised as being one of the hardest disciplines in sport. So be prepared.

The first item of equipment you will need, is a pair of bag gloves. And at this point I would advise you to look for quality rather than economy. Although you might think you are saving money, a cheap pair of bag gloves will fall apart in no time at all.

Next comes a pair of bandages or hand wraps, which I will show you how to wrap in the next chapter.

A skipping rope is an excellent form of fitness training, and good for hand - foot co-ordination. There are lots of ropes on the market, I would recommend a leather rope for durability.

Although a pair of boxing boots are not essential, they are well recommended to stop sprained ankles.

The Art of Boxing

The type of clothing you wear depends on you. Most types of sports clothing would be fine, providing, they don't restrict your movement. As you start to become more relaxed and confident with your style, you can progress on to a pair of boxing shorts.

A punch bag is the next thing to look at. The types of bags available are endless, I would just say, don't be taken in on price. The weight of the bag should be at least, 25 kilos. Remember, you might not be hitting it that hard at the moment, but before long, you'll be punching two or three times as hard, and you'll need a heavy bag to take the pounding.

A punch ball, or floor to ceiling, as some people call it is an excellent piece of equipment to help with hand - eye co-ordination, as well as speed and reflexes. But be patient, the punch ball takes a lot of getting used to.

The speed ball, again a very good aid to hand - eye co-ordination, as well as strengthening upper arms and shoulders. As with the punch ball, be patient.

As you progress to partner work, you will need a pair of pads for your partner to wear. Leather or canvas are just as good

When you eventually start to spar, you will need a pair of 16 oz sparring gloves, a gum shield, groin guard, and a head guard. These items are all very important, as they actually stop you from getting hurt, so take your time and look for quality.

CHAPTER TWO
Safety

As with any sport, especially contact sports, safety is paramount. Not only from your point of view, but also your sparring partners and the people using the gym with you. Never misuse the equipment in the gym and never under any circumstances punch a piece of equipment with your bare hand.

Many people from the martial arts world say that by punching bricks or boards, you actually toughen your knuckles. This may well be the case, but what's the point of having one inch thick calluses on your knuckle's, when they are rapped in sixteen ounces of foam?. Trust me, if you haven't got a good punch, the size of your knuckles will make no difference whatsoever to your ability to knock someone out.

It is important to warm up before your work out, this will help to stop miner injuries and strains. Don't neglect this part of your training, it is probably the most important part of your workout.

As you progress with your training, you will start to work with a partner, using pads. Be careful, as your accuracy might not be as good as you think. Give your partner a chance to improve with you.

Sparring

Eventually, you will move on to sparring, which will be a completely different experience to anything you will have done up to that point. The whole point of sparring, is to put into practice, what you have learned in the gym. If you are not a member of a boxing club, you might need to find a suitably qualified sparring partner to help you. But remember, the point of sparring is to practice your skills on a moving target, and as you will learn, a target that hits back is a lot more difficult to hit. Don't get carried away with your punching. At this point technique is the most important thing.

Bandaging Your Hands

Although you won't be punching with all of your body weight just yet, it's still a good idea to start to use bandages under your bag gloves. There are lots of different ways to wrap your hands, for instance, if you have particularly weak wrists, you would pay more attention to them when putting your bandages on and take more wraps around your wrist to support them. But let's concentrate on the basic technique to start with.

To start the process, open your hand flat with your fingers straight and apart. Most bandages these days have a ready made loop to put your thumb through, but if yours haven't, just cut a small whole in the end and slip your thumb through. Keeping your fingers and thumb out strait, start to rap the bandage around your wrist. Be careful not to pull the bandage to tight, remember, once the bandage is on you have to pull on a pair of gloves and then clench your fist, so just remember, you are not supporting a broken wrist. After a couple of times around your wrist, start to move up towards your knuckles, don't be too worried about

Safety

overlapping your knuckles, when you form a fist the bandage will be pulled back. Wrap the knuckles four or five times, then start to move back towards the wrist, zig zaging backwards and forwards, pay special attention to the wrist joint, and then finish off by wrapping up to about five or six inches along the arm. As with most things so far, this is new to you, so don't expect it to be perfect first time. One important point, if the bandage is too tight, take it off and start again, a tight bandage will restrict blood flow to the hand and cause a lot of pain. It is important that your hands feel comfortable as well as safe. See figs 1 to 5.

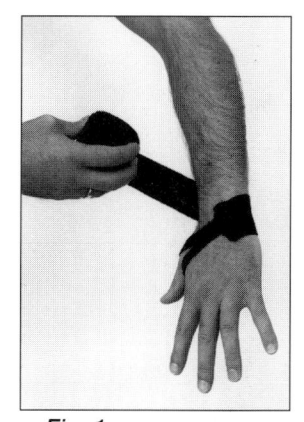

Fig. 1.

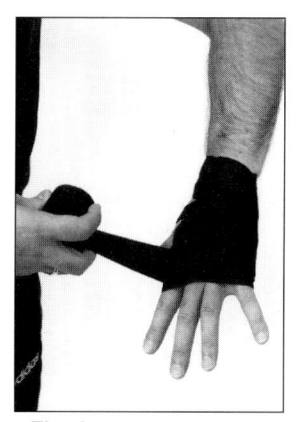

Fig. 2.

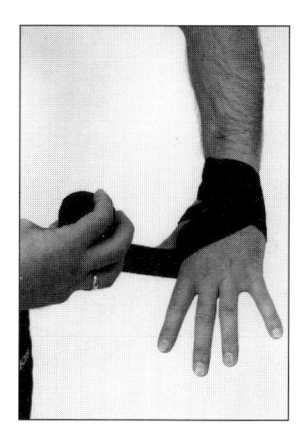

Fig. 3.

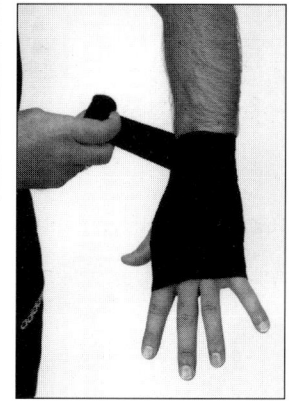

Fig. 4.

Fig. 5.

The Art of Boxing

CHAPTER THREE
Stance

Balance

Boxing, as with any sport starts and ends with a good Stance. Before you read on, think for a minute, a tennis player waiting to receive a serve, a goal keeper waiting for a penalty to be taken, a golfer teeing up for a drive. Also look at the Martial Arts world, Thai Boxers, Karateka, Judo players and Wrestlers, worlds apart in their approach to fighting but all sharing one thing in common, BALANCE.

Imagine a Judo player trying to through an opponent over his shoulder while being off balance, they would both end up in a heap on the floor. The same with a Karate fighter, how could he possibly kick his opponent if he was off balance. Get the picture? Balance is everything. If you haven't got a good solid base to work from, you might as well pack your bags and go home.

Southpaws

Before I begin I should say a few words about left handed people, or as we say in the trade 'south paws'. Traditionally a right handed person stood with his left foot in front of his right, and vice versa for a left handed person. The reasoning behind this was that a right handed boxer

The Art of Boxing

would use his left hand or Jab to set his opponent up for the "big" right cross, this being his stronger arm. Obviously the opposite would apply for a left handed person. However more and more people, myself included are taking the view that with the correct training a Boxer should be able to fight in either stance. I am one of the fortunate few who can. I am naturally ambidextrous, 'what ever that means'. All I will say to you at this point, is stick to what feels comfortable.

As right handed people out number left handed people, I will just ask you lefties to bear with me, as we go along you'll soon get used to swapping my instructions around.

'A Good Solid Base'

So, what do we consider to be a 'good solid base'?, and what's more how can we keep this solid base as we attack and defend? Well that's the hard bit, but don't despair, at the end of this chapter, you will have a much better understanding of what stance is all about.

Standing with your feet shoulder with apart, step forward about eighteen inches with your left foot. (that's your right foot if you are a south paw, get the idea) it is imperative that you feel comfortable and 'balanced', everything we do from now on is based on this position, which we will call the *ready position.* See fig 6.

Fig. 6.

Stance

Fig. 6a. *Fig. 6b.*

Standing in the **ready** position, turn your left shoulder towards your opponent. It might help if you stand in front of a mirror, you can use your own reflection as your opponent. Now bend your arms, bringing your left hand to shoulder level in front of you. Your right hand should be at the same height at the side your chin. Lower your chin to your shoulder and look through your eyebrows. It's important to note at this point, that the natural thing to do as you lift your arms and lower your chin, is to round your shoulders. However, this will have the effect of constricting movement and taking three or four inches off your height, so keeping in your original position, stand up straight, you should feel much better and more confident. See fig 7 (next page).

The Art of Boxing

The first thing you will be thinking is, "This is uncomfortable". This is a natural feeling as you are in a position which is alien to you, don't worry, you'll soon get used to it. At this stage, you don't need to pay too much attention to what your hands are doing, your mind will be more than occupied with what your feet are doing.

Fig. 7.

Adding Movement

Before you start to move, just bend your knees a little, this will give you more bounce as you move around, and more leverage when you start to punch. The basic movements we will go through are, backwards and forwards, and left and right. Starting by going forward, first move your front foot forward about six to eight inches, then bring your back foot forward the same distance, this will bring you back to your original

Stance

position. Now start to move forward two or three steps at a time and then move back the same distance, starting with your back foot first then bringing your front foot back to the start position. Well done! Now you know how to do a good impression of a 'Mummy' on the war path.

Lets look at what we are doing. At the moment, you are probable stepping backwards and forwards, using mechanical 'one - two' motions. As you become more familiar with the movement, you should start to slide your feet backwards and forwards as opposed to stepping.

To help you to do this, try to transfer some of your weight from foot to foot. As you start to move forward, transfer some of your weight on to your back foot, this will help you to 'Push' off your back foot giving more emphasis to the movement.

The same principal applies to your front foot as you move back. Transferring some of your weight to your front foot will allow you to push off your front foot. The process of transferring your weight from foot to foot gives the movement more fluency and a sliding motion, as opposed to a mechanical 'step'.

Now lets look at sideward movement. The same principal applies to sideways movement as to backwards and forwards. Start by sliding your front foot six to eight inches to the left, then bringing the back foot across the same distance, ending up in the start position. The same thing for the back foot, slide your foot across six to eight inches, then bring your front foot across to the start position. As with the first move, your movements will become more fluent as you start to transfer some of your weight from foot to foot as you move.

The Art of Boxing

As you go through your drill in front of the mirror, you will probably start to think to yourself, "Why doesn't Prince Nassem move up and down like this?". Well the truth is all good Boxers including Prince Nassem, started in exactly the same way as you, what you are looking at when you see the top professionals dancing around the ring with no effort is the result of countless hours, practising in front of the mirror.

As you get used to moving around in your stance, you will begin to get the idea of just how important footwork is to the boxer. There is no point in having a big KO punch, if you can't get to your opponent to land it, and just as important, being able to get out of the way of danger.

Dancing

As my students start to progress with their footwork, I start to introduce them to some of the finer points of foot work. It is difficult for the novice boxer to understand that it is perfectly normal to actually 'Dance' while training, continually changing direction, avoiding imaginary punches and counter attacking. I always have to smile as I watch my novice fighters going through their paces feeling so self conscious, remember what I said before, boxing is very personal, and the person laughing at you as you go through your paces won't be the one taking the punches, you will.

I always tell a novice boxer to try to have patience with what he is doing, once you start to understand and feel comfortable with the basics, then and only then should you start to allow your own personality to play a part in what you are doing. Although it is true to say that at this point, you should start to feel a part of what you are doing, it is important to go back to the basics every now and then, remember, no one's perfect and bad habits can start to creep in without anyone noticing.

Shadow boxing is the best way to improve your foot work, so make sure you spend enough time each session working in front of the mirror.

CHAPTER FOUR
Basic Punches

The Jab

So, now we've learned to float like a butterfly, we need to look at the stinging bit. The Jab. Probably the most under-estimated punch in the book. The Jab is the punch you use to set up an attack, the punch you use to score a point if your opponent drops his guard, the punch you use to break your opponents rhythm, making it very difficult for him to launch an attack, and the punch you use to keep your opponent at bay while you take a much needed breather.

As you can imagine, the jab can be used defensively or offensively, going forward or going back.

To launch an attack you would use a strong powerful jab, keeping your opponent busy, whilst a fast snappy jab would be used to break up an oncoming attack.

As you progress you will also see how the jab can be used to 'feign' your opponent, pulling him off balance and opening him up for an attack.

The Art of Boxing

Starting in the ready position, punch with the front hand, or, the jab. Although the jab can be used in many different ways, the punch actually varies very little. The best way to describe the jab is, 'the quickest way between two points is a straight line'. Your arm is a piston that can only move in a straight line, the only variation being the speed.

Keeping your weight evenly balanced and your guard up, punch in a straight line, as your arm straightens, turn your fist in a clockwise direction, this will give added strength to your punch, in effect, 'drilling' your punch home. **See fig 8**.

Fig. 8.

This exercise, like most others should be practised in front of a mirror. I've already said how important the mirror is and as you improve, you will come to appreciate the mirror as one of your most important training aides.

Shadow boxing

Here I should mention one or two things about 'shadow boxing'. Firstly it is dangerous to throw full blown punches into thin air. The only time a punch should be thrown at full strength is when there is

Basic Punches

something to absorb the power and take the impact. Throwing a full blown punch into thin air will cause the elbow and shoulder joints to 'snap' open. This makes shadow boxing quite difficult for the novice as it is very hard for a boxer to 'pull' a punch, but as before, be patient, practice makes perfect.

Secondly, unlike bag work which tends to keep the boxer in one place, shadow boxing allows the boxer to develop his hand and foot co-ordination and also to allow him to explore the physics of the ring, developing and using angles etc.

Fig. 9.

To make the jab more effective, the next thing to do, is to step in with the punch. This is done with the front foot. As you throw the jab, step forward about six inches with your front foot, then step back to the ready position. The object of this is to bring you into range and then out again. **See fig 9.**

You will now understand the importance of good footwork, being light on your feet is imperative if you are going to keep ahead of your opponent, as you can see from the photograph, the movement is short and fast, but very effective.

The Art of Boxing

The Right Hand

As with any punch you throw, the right hand is used to score points by landing cleanly on the target. However, the right hand is also one of the most effective KO punches. If the right hand is thrown correctly, it is absolutely devastating. There is a lot of misconception about the right hand, namely, the harder you throw it the better it is, this is complete nonsense. The secret to a powerful punch, is a combination of speed and leverage.

The power behind a right hand, comes from a good solid base, allowing the hips to spin around, which then whiplash the upper body, sending the punch on its way with lightning speed. **See fig 10.**

Imagine you have a pole going through the centre of your body, like a hobby horse on a merry go round.

Now, from the ready position throw the right hand slowly making sure you don't go forward, remember, you are anchored to the floor with a metal pole. The only movement you can make, is to spin around in an anti-clockwise direction. See fig 11 (next page).

Fig. 10.

26

Basic Punches

When the right hand is fully extended, your right shoulder should be turned towards your opponent. Like the jab, you can increase the power of the punch, by turning the fist in an anti clockwise direction as the punch lands. Once the right hand is fully extended, you can then recoil like a spring and return to the original position. At this stage you should not be using any forward motion, the object of the exercise is to teach you to use your hips and turn on an axis. We will be introducing forward motion later.

Fig. 11.

Combining The Punches

Now we can put the two punches together. Starting with the jab, throw the punch as before. As the punch is pulled back, start to spin your body around in an anti clockwise direction, releasing the right hand, once the punch is fully extended, return to the ready position. See fig 12-13 (next page).

The Art of Boxing

Fig. 13.

Fig. 12.

It's now time to put everything together. As you probably already know, boxers always train by working in rounds. The length of the round can vary between two and three minutes. Some people seem to think that training with four or five minute rounds increases stamina and although this is probably true, what it also does is slow the work rate down. So when a boxer who has been training using four minute rounds comes up against a boxer who is used to training using three minutes rounds the boxer with the higher work rate will inevitably come out on top. Namely the one used to training with three minute rounds.

Basic Punches

You should now be starting to use your imagination to 'Shadow Box' with your fictitious opponent, dancing around the ring jabbing as you move, setting him up for a right hand, then moving away. Try to use some 'one - two' combinations remembering to turn as you throw your punches. If you are feeling comfortable, try six or eight punch combo's, but make sure you keep your balance and remember it's important to enjoy what you are doing, so don't take yourself to seriously, its early days yet. The most important thing at this stage, is technique, and I cannot emphasise enough, the importance of practice.

CHAPTER FIVE
Defence

Of course, throwing punches at a punch bag is the easy bit. The problems begin when, the punch bag starts to hit back. This opens the novice up to a whole new world. Instead of just throwing punches, he has to start to think about the consequences. And I can tell you from experience, there's nothing like a stiff right hand on the nose to make you think. **"What the bloody hell am I doing here?"**. So the first thing to remember is that every attack has a defence.

Lets look at some of the options. The humble jab can be defended in so many ways I could write a book on that subject alone, but to keep things nice and simple, we'll look at some of the basics. The main point to remember about straight punches, is that you can see them coming. You'll understand that better as we go on. So bearing that in mind, the easiest way to defend against a jab, is to parry the punch.

This process is so often over played and yet it is the most simple defence in the book. As you stand in the ready position, imagine your opponent throwing a jab straight at your chin. You should keep still and don't move away from the punch, this is a natural think to do, but as your confidence grows, you will feel less inclined to do this. As the punch comes toward you, start to move your right hand across to the left

The Art of Boxing

to meet it. As the punch reaches you, deflect the punch over your left shoulder. The only movement you need, is a twist of the wrist as the punch connects with your glove. It is important to remember that you are not trying to stop the punch, only to deflect it by using it's own momentum. See fig 14.

Fig. 14.

The amount of effort needed to parry a punch is minimal, which is why it is rarely practised. Don't neglect your parrying when you are shadow boxing, remember, the more you practice, the more natural the process becomes. The right hand is parried in just the same way. As the right hand is thrown, the punch is parried over the right shoulder by the left hand. Remember, the punch is being deflected over your right shoulder, not stopped in its tracks. See fig 15.

Fig. 15.

Defence

Slipping The Punch

Another form of defence, is to slip the punch. The punch can be slipped inside or outside, depending on how confident you are feeling.

Starting with the jab. As the jab is thrown, bend forward and to the right at the same time, as you do this the punch will carry on over your left shoulder. Don't bend too far, only far enough to miss the punch.

Fig. 16.

The same thing goes for the right hand. As the right hand is thrown, bend forward and to the left, the punch will continue over your right shoulder. Even though you have evaded the punch, keep your guard up. The original punch might have been a feign. These two moves will take you to the outside of the punch, as you can see from figs 16 & 17.

Fig. 17.

The Art of Boxing

The same principal applies to slipping inside the punch. As the jab is thrown, bend to the left, bending the front knee and twisting to the left as you drop.

As the right hand is thrown, bend to the right, turning your left shoulder slightly to the right as you do. Unlike slipping to the outside of a punch, which takes you out of punching range.

Fig. 18.

Slipping inside the punch takes you into firing range, as you are turning onto your opponents punches.

So it is important to make sure you keep your guard held high.

See figs 18 & 19.

Fig. 19.

Defence

Practice these moves continually, as you can see, your reaction to the punch must be at least as fast as the punch being thrown. As you become more comfortable with the move, start to transfer some of your body weight on to your front foot. This will put you in a better position to counter attack with uppercuts, as we will discuss later.

Ducking The Punch

A very simple and under used defence, which can be used against hooks as well as straight punches, is to duck under the punch. There are different ways to do this. For the novice boxer, the most effective way to duck under the punch, is to bend at the knees as the punch is thrown, dropping in a straight line with your weight balanced evenly over your feet. It is important to note, you only need to drop far enough to let the punch go over your head. See fig 20.

Fig. 20.

Leaning Back (The Lay Back)

The forth evasive move we are going to look at is probably the most difficult to master. Not because of its complicated manoeuvres, but because unlike the other moves, you are going to be slightly off balance.

The Art of Boxing

The same manoeuvre is used to defend against a left or right hand. As the punch is thrown, lean back, bending your back knee as you do. Don't lean too far, only far enough to avoid you punch. See fig 21.

Fig. 21.

As you can see, this is a very effective move, as it takes your head out of punching range, but leaves your feet in the original position, therefore making counter attacking more effective. As you move your head and upper body backwards, you are giving the effect of moving your whole body out of range, therefore pulling your opponent on to your punches. As you become more practised with the move, try taking a small step backwards with your back foot, this will make the counter attack even easier to mount. See fig 22.

Fig. 22.

As you practice these moves, you will start to see the importance of continually moving your head and body as you throw punches. It is probably a bit difficult to put everything together at the moment, but as I have already said, keep practising, and remember, as you go through your paces, the top professionals you watch on the television are doing exactly the same thing.

Defending Hooks and Uppercuts

Hooks and Uppercuts, are the hardest punches to defend against. The reason for this, is because they appear from the edge of your vision. To demonstrate what I mean, look straight ahead and hold your finger out in front of you. Now, keep looking straight ahead and at the same time start to move your finger in an ark to the side. Keep looking straight ahead. At the point where your finger starts to disappear, stop. As you are looking ahead, imagine a hook coming straight at you from the direction of your finger, hard enough to defend against in itself. But, imagine your opponent coming at you throwing a one two combination, as you parry the left and try to counter the right, out of the blue, something hits you on the side of the head and starts bells ringing in your ear.

You have just been stung with a left hook, and you didn't even see it coming. Peripheral vision is vital to a boxer for this very reason, so keep your wits about you and watch your opponents hands. As you can imagine, defending against a hook or uppercut is very difficult. The best form of defence is to evade the punch, by slipping or ducking it. If you don't have time to do this, cover up by holding your hand up to your head, with your elbow tucked into your side. See figs 23 & 24 (next page).

The Art of Boxing

Fig. 23.

Fig. 24.

CHAPTER SIX
Hooks and Uppercuts

First things first, congratulations on getting this far. Its not quite as easy as it looks is it. So, we've looked at stance and some basic punches. This is where the fun really starts. Hopefully, you will have gained enough confidence with your foot work to be able to dance all over the gym. So we'll start by going right back to the beginning.

Unlike straight punches, which can be unloaded 'straight from the hip', you can shoot a right hand out in exactly the same way a gun shoots a bullet, hooks and uppercuts need to be looked at from a completely different angle. Remember when we talked about being anchored to the floor like a hobby horse, well if you didn't get the idea then, you soon will.

The Basic Principle

The variations on a hook, and indeed an uppercut are endless. So, let's look at the basic principal. Firstly, and probably most importantly, the hook is aimed at the side of the head, as opposed to the front, as with

The Art of Boxing

a straight left or right. This has the effect of spinning the head sideways which causes the brain to hit against the side of the head and ultimately cause a KO. Although a punch to the front of the head can be just as effective, because the head is being spun around as opposed to being knocked back onto a strong set of neck muscles, the resistance is nowhere near as strong.

It is worth noting, that it is very difficult to launch a hook from a standing start. In other words, a hook is best thrown 'behind' another punch, for instance, a straight right, followed by a left hook. If you think about what we have been practising so far, the reasoning behind this should become obvious.

The Left Hook to the Head

Fig. 25.

As before, you should be well balanced, with your weight spread evenly over both feet. As we go through the punch, try not to put too much weight on your front foot, remember, balance is everything. From the ready position, turn your left hand, right if you are a south paw, (don't worry I haven't forgotten you southpaws) toward you, as if you are looking at something inside your palm. Now lift your elbow up until it has reached a position of ninety degrees to your body. See fig 25 (previous page).

As you can see, the starting position of the punch is completely different from that of a straight punch. From this position, and remember, you are pivoting on an imaginary pole going through the Centre of your body, turn slowly to the right. The first thing you will notice, is that there is no stopping point. The further you twist, the further you go around. Of course in reality, your opponents chin will stop you before you go to far. 'at least that's the theory'. The main point to remember about a hook is that, it is not an uppercut, nor a bowl-over punch. The hand is neither coming up nor going down, but travelling in a perfect circle at ninety degrees to your body.

The reason I say this, is because I have had many conversations with 'armchair ' experts about the 'Hook'. As you can see from Fig 26. As the hook is thrown, the elbow is following in a straight line behind the fist, and in turn the shoulder is following in a straight line behind the elbow. One or two people I have met, argue that the punch should be thrown, with the palm facing down. The problem with this punch, is that as the elbow follows through, it will start to raise itself higher than the fist, turning it into a bowl over punch. The bowl over punch

Fig. 26.

The Art of Boxing

is a very effective punch, when thrown at short range. However, the stance and body positioning for a bowl over punch are completely different to that of a hook.

The one big problem for the novice puncher when throwing a hook, is the range. That is the distance the target is from the punch and with a hook, the nearer the better. The reason for this is that the hook is using the spinning motion of the body for it's effect. The shorter the hook, the more power is passed from the body through the arm. If the arm is too long, the effect will be lost. **See figs 27 & 28.**

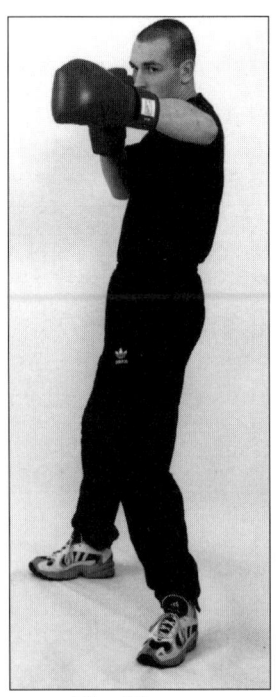

Fig. 27.   *Fig. 28.*

As you start to throw the hook, you will probably be tempted to drop your arm to your side and 'wind' the punch up. This is understandable, as I said earlier, the hook is a very difficult punch to throw from a standing

Hooks and Uppercuts

start. Try not to get into this habit from the start, because, by dropping your hand you are exposing your own chin to your opponent, and more importantly, turning your short powerful hook into a long sweeping 'slap'. See fig 29.

Start to introduce the hook into your training and use it in your combo's. Remember to keep your hands high, it's easy to let your hand drop ready to throw the hook, this will have the effect of telling your opponent what you are about to do. At this stage I would advise you to keep to your front hand, that's left for orthodox, right for southpaws. Although the principle for throwing a hook with your back hand is basically the same, the footwork involved is slightly different.

Fig. 29.

The Left Hook to the Body

Hooking to the body, is much the same as hooking to the head, the obvious difference being the height. So, unlike a left hook to the head. To throw a left hook to the body, you first have to drop your hand. This has obvious hazards attached to it, namely, your chin is left wide open to an attack, so be very careful not to take too long.

The Art of Boxing

Start in the *ready* position, keeping your chin tucked in, out of danger, lower your hand to just above waist level, and turn your palm towards you. As with hooks to the head, the punch is thrown at close range, so don't extend your arm, keep your elbow close to your body and let your hips do all the work. Spin around and snap your hips, whiplashing your arm. See fig 30.

Fig. 30.

Right Hook to the Body

The same goes for the right hand, by dropping your hand to deliver the punch, you are exposing your chin, so make the move fast and effective. Lower your hand to just above your waist, turning your palm inward, as before keep your elbow close to your side and spin around using your own body weight to create the power. See fig 31 (next page).

Hooks and Uppercuts

As you get used to the idea of spinning as you throw a hook, you will start to feel a lot less awkward and much looser. This in turn will allow you to start to put your body behind the punch. As you put different combo's together, you will begin to start to shift your weight from side to side, and from front to back.

Fig. 31.

This will give a far more fluent and flowing motion to your punching. Being free from the rigidity of the novice, you can now start to experiment with lots of different combo's, and even styles. But remember to come back to the basic's now and then. Bad habits form easily.

The uppercut is another strange beast. It should be given as much respect as the hook. Like the hook, if the uppercut is thrown and misses, you can be left off balance, therefore vulnerable to an attack. So for the time being, we'll keep the punch at short range, again like the hook, this will give the punch better leverage and more power.

The Art of Boxing

Fig. 32.

Left Uppercut

Starting in the *ready* position, don't forget to keep your weight evenly spread, turn your left hand, so you are looking at your palm. From this position, thrust your fist upwards towards your opponents chin, at an angle of about thirty degrees to your body. Keep your elbow close to your body and let your hips do the work. See fig 32.

Right Uppercut

Using the same principle, you should be aiming the punch underneath your opponents chin forcing his head backwards. Remember to keep your hooks and uppercuts 'tight'. These punches are close range punches using the leverage your body provides naturally. You can now start to put combinations together using four or five different punches. See fig 33.

Fig. 33.

Feigning Your Opponent

As you go through your shadow boxing, start to introduce the odd feign, 'and no I don't mean fall over'. Looking in the mirror, pretend to throw a jab, this will draw your opponent off guard, because he is expecting you to throw the punch, he will start to parry with his right hand, which in turn will leave his chin exposed. Now as he parries the imaginary jab, throw your right hand and follow up with a left hook.

CHAPTER SEVEN
Combinations

We've spoken about combinations fairly loosely up to now, so lets take a closer look. Obviously, it is always to your advantage if you can land a number of punches as opposed to a one off.

There is a big danger in looking for that big KO punch at the cost of a good work rate. Although it is true to say that every punch you throw should be thrown with total commitment or 'bad intention', as we say, there is no guarantee of a KO at any time in a fight. So that leaves us with a high work rate with good quality punches.

Effective Combinations

So how do we use combo's effectively? Well to start with, we don't go running out at the beginning of the first round with all guns blazing. Remember, you might be feeling fit and strong, but so is your opponent, so work your way into the fight. Cast your mind back to our work with the jab. By now you should be firing your jab off with devastating speed and accuracy. Work behind your jab all of the time, continually lining your opponent up.

Watching novice fighters going through their paces in the ring, the first thing you notice is that they 'Go to the head' far too often. As I said before, it's pointless, and dangerous, looking for that 'big one', if the opening comes, you'll see it and act accordingly. The idea of combination punching is to land lots of good quality punches to the head AND body. These punches will start to wear your opponent down making him weaker as the fight continues.

Variety

The other important point about combo's, is that the more variety of punches you use the more confusing it will be for you opponent. Imagine having to defend against a jab, straight right, left hook, right uppercut, left uppercut and right hook, one after the other. If your opponent knows what you are going to throw next, you might as well lay down and take the count. The object of all those hours continuously shadow boxing, is to make it second nature for you to throw lots of different punches one after the other.

One of the unique things about boxing, is the way a fighter can 'go with the flow', whether he is coming forward in attack or going back in defence, the ability to throw punches from any angle, in any combination is a wonderful sight to behold.

Looking for the Finish

Sooner or later, if you are continually throwing lots of good quality combo's your opponent will start to get fed up eating your leather and begin to loose heart and if a fighter has no heart, then he has nothing. It is now that you should start to look for the Finish, working your weak, tired and empty opponent into a corner, leaving him with nowhere to go. Then and only then have you got the fight completely under control, you can now open up with your hardest, fastest punches throwing from every angle.

The one big danger of opening up with a combination, is the possibility of a counter attack, which we will talk about later. It's easy to forget about defence in the middle of an attack. Always remember to keep your hands up to protect yourself.

I have got a golden rule about hand positioning. That is, if the hand is not on it's way to a target, or on it's way back, then it is wrapped around your chin keeping it safe.

Flowing with the Punch

As you progress with your combination work, you will begin to appreciate the importance of body movement. There are so many different punches being thrown from so many different angles, the positioning of your feet is very important. As you go through your shadow boxing routines, start to role with the punches, transferring your weight from foot to foot as you throw the punch. At the same time start to throw combinations going forward and moving back.

You'll see how hard it is punching while going back, or on your back foot, as opposed to going forward on your front foot. Although we have seen how important it is to keep your weight balanced evenly on both feet, you are now starting to realise the importance of transferring your weight from foot to foot as you throw different punches.

In the **ready** position, start by throwing a left, right, left hook, right uppercut. Try throwing the combo a few times without moving your hips.

The Art of Boxing

Keep your whole body rigid as you throw the punches. You can see how ineffective the punches are when they are thrown on their own. The punches become disjointed and mechanical, with no continuity to them.

Now throw the same combo, but this time start to move your hips as you throw each punch. Start with the left jab, as you throw the jab, snap your left hip forward at the same time. As the punch returns and you start to throw the right, do the same with your right hip. If this feels a bit strange, try throwing an imaginary left right, but snapping your hips as if you had. While you throw the imaginary punches look down at your hips and take note of their movement, or lack of, as the case may be. The exercise you are going through can make or break a combination. If you can't flow with your punches, you will become static and predictable.

As I have said before, shadow boxing should be used to practice these body movements, over and over again, repetition is the only way to perfect their complicated moves.

So now try throwing the same four punch combo again, this time snapping your hips as you throw each punch. Can you feel the difference in the power, instead of being disjointed, your whole body is working as one, throwing the punch effortlessly.

As you become more comfortable with combination punching, and don't be too impatient, you can start to experiment with different attacks. Working to the body and head and back to the body, hooking, jabbing, uppercutting etc. This is where the fun starts.

Combinations

As you go through your routine in front of the mirror, try to think of as many combo's as you can. You might be surprised at how many different combo's you can produce using the basic punches you have learned.

Combo 1

To get you started, take a look at some of these three and four punch combo's and take it from there. **Figs 34 to 37** show a jab - right cross - left hook - right uppercut to the head. Notice the combination starts with straight punches and as you go forward, you bring yourself into range for the hook and uppercut.

Fig. 34.

Fig. 35.

The Art of Boxing

Fig. 36.

Fig. 37.

Combo 2

Figs 38 to 40 (next page) show a right hand to the body - left hook - right uppercut to the head. This combo is an ideal counter attack to a right hand. The reason for punching to the body with the right hand, is to drop

Combinations

your opponent's hands, thus opening up his chin for the hook. Don't forget to step in when you punch.

Fig. 38.

Fig. 39.

Fig. 40.

The Art of Boxing

Combo 3

Figs 41 to 44 show a jab to the head - right to the body - left uppercut - right uppercut to the head. Again, notice the way the combo changes from head to body and back to the head again. This makes defending very difficult.

Fig. 41.

Fig. 42.

Combinations

Fig. 43.

Fig. 44.

The Art of Boxing

Combo 4

Figs 45 to 48 show a left hook to the body - left hook to the head - right uppercut to the head - left hook to the head. This combo would obviously be used when you had already worked your way inside your opponent's defence. The idea of throwing a left hook to the body and then the head, is to open up your opponent's chin by punching him in the ribs making him flinch, and dropping his guard.

Fig. 45.

Fig. 46.

Combinations

Fig. 47.

Fig. 48.

The Art of Boxing

CHAPTER EIGHT
Advanced Footwork

Range

One of the hardest things for a boxer to master, is range. That is, the distance you should be from your opponent in order to land your punches. You might think this would be easy, just keep going forward until you are in range. Of course this is completely wrong, as you will see when you start to spar, that's if you haven't started already.

If you pay particular attention to a boxer during a fight, you will notice that a lot of the time he is actually out of range. This is deliberate. As I have said already, a boxer must be able to fight going forwards and backwards, which is the way a fight goes. So as a fighter starts to mount an attack, he will work his way into range using his jab, put together one or more combinations and then move out of danger. Of course as one fighter is doing this, so is his opponent, which is where things start to get a bit complicated.

A lot of the finer points of boxing are completely missed by the general public because they just don't see what the boxer is doing. You should

The Art of Boxing

be starting to look at things from a fighters point of few, and looking at things in much more depth. Try concentrating on a fighters feet instead of his hands, and you will see what I mean.

Watching a fight progress, you will notice how the tempo of the fight changes, as one fighter attacks and defends. So you should now begin to appreciate the importance of good footwork. We are going to do a couple of exercise's in front of the mirror putting combinations and footwork together.

Hand - Foot Co-ordination

Start by throwing a four punch combo and at the same time, go forward and attack your opponent. The first thing you will notice, is that your hands and feet are out of sink. Now do the same thing again, this time in slow motion. Start with the jab. As you throw your left hand, step forward with your left foot. Now throw your right hand and step forward with your right foot. This will bring you back to the original position, but remember the bit in the middle, your hips should still be providing all of the power.

From the *ready* position start by throwing a jab, step forward with your left foot, but instead of stepping straight forward, step forward and slightly to the left. Now bring your right foot forward as before throwing the right hand as you do. This will put you in a perfect position to throw a left hook. Throw the left hook and snap your hips at the same time.

You will notice that although you have thrown three punches, you have only stepped forward twice. The reason for this is because you put yourself in the right position to throw a left hook by stepping forward and throwing your right hand. But more importantly, you should not throw a hook with only one foot on the floor, remember, you are spinning your body around as you throw the punch and need to be well anchored to give yourself the proper leverage.

Angles

By stepping across your opponent as opposed to going straight forward, you are creating an angle. This is an important part of attacking with combinations. The reason being, if you were to go forward in a straight line you would be 'walking on' to your opponents punches. By stepping across your opponent, you are making it more difficult for him to hit you and at the same time making it easier for you to hit him.

Move forward in front of the mirror zig-zagging from side to side as you go. As you improve and become more confident with your foot work, you will start to appreciate how much your feet play a part in your ability to box with skill and accuracy.

By now you should be spending as much time on practising footwork as you do on punching. As you go through your paces try to continually create angles whilst attacking, and averting an attack by moving from side to side, making it very difficult for your opponent to keep his rhythm.

Dancing

Earlier in the book, I spoke about 'Dancing' in front of the mirror, you should now be beginning to understand just what I meant. I can't emphasise enough, the importance of good footwork, you can never spend to much time practising with imaginary opponents, continually

The Art of Boxing

attacking and defending. It is generally acknowledged that an illusive fighter is by far the hardest type of fighter to box. Try playing some music and dancing along.

As you start to understand the finer points of footwork, you will begin to see how it can be quite easy to elude an attack from your opponent just by moving your back foot ninety degrees to the left or springing backwards off your front foot, leaving your opponent over stretched.

It is worth remembering, you are going to be fighting in a 'Square' ring so it is important you get used to the idea of moving out of danger and not letting yourself be put into a corner. The golden rule is always try to stand in the Centre of the ring and make your opponent do all the work. Much the same as playing squash, the player in the Centre of the court has control of the game, making his opponent do all the running.

CHAPTER NINE
Partner Work

Up until this point, you have been working on your own, getting used to the basics and forming that all important boxing brain. Now we can move on to the next stage. That is, partner work. This kind of training can be very rewarding to the boxer, and the learning curve should start to accelerate.

How do you choose your partner? The most important point is that your partner must be willing to help you improve your skills, not by unnecessary criticism, but helpful comments. Your partner may not have the same knowledge or experience as you. So who ever you choose must be patient.

More times than not, your partner is only assisting you in a particular move or exercise. An example of this would be to ask your partner to throw a jab, enabling you to parry or counter the punch. But don't forget, your partner is not a walking punch bag, so be gentle with him.

Pad Work

Probably the most beneficial kind of partner work is pad work. There are lots of different names given to the pads, such as, hook and jab pads,

The Art of Boxing

target pads, focus mitts and so on. I'm sure you will know what I am talking about, when I describe pad work.

The most important thing for your partner, or 'pad-man' to remember, is that like bag work you are throwing full blown punches, and as I said before, it is imperative for the punch to connect with something substantial. Therefore, the pad-man must get used to 'Catching' the punch and taking the full impact. The pad-man must never try to out smart the boxer by pulling the pad away at the last second. This would serve no purpose whatsoever, and would probably do the fighter a lot of damage. As you and your pad-man get used to each other, and become more confidant, you can start to put lots of combinations together, using your feet to come forward and go back as you punch.

The most effective way to do this, is for your pad-man to call the shots you are going to throw. i.e., one two, one two left hook, right cross left hook etc.

The positioning of the pads is very important. The pads should be held facing towards the boxer. To take a hook, the pad is turned towards the oncoming punch. See fig 51.

Fig. 51.

Partner Work

The most effective way to throw punches at the pads, is to hit the opposite pad to your punch. That is, the left hand is thrown at the right pad, and the right hand is thrown at the left pad. This goes for hooks and uppercuts as well as straight punches. See figs. 52 & 53.

Fig. 51.

Fig. 52.

The reasoning behind this, is to make the boxer turn through the axis, making the punch more effective. As you can see in both cases, the shoulder of the punching arm is facing towards the pad-man, showing a fully committed punch. As the pad-man becomes more familiar with the boxer, and how he works, he can start to give the odd reminder when the boxers defence becomes ragged.

The Art of Boxing

He can do this by giving the boxer a gentle tap on the side of the head if he drops his guard. But take note, the point of the tap, is to remind the boxer to keep his guard up, not to knock him out! I have seen on many occasions, the pad-man doing his best to catch the boxer out with a hard slap if the punch was not delivered fast enough.

Fig. 54.

Rather than improving the boxers technique, this often has the reverse effect. The boxer will start to throw his punches short in anticipation of being hit by the pad-man. Although you might think this is good practice, you are quite wrong.

Fig. 55.

The whole point of pad work, is to allow the boxer to fine hone his punching, and not give the pad-man easy target practice.

Pad work improves hand speed and accuracy, the pad being about the same size as a human head. Pad work should also drastically improve a fighters foot work.

As the pad-man attacks and defends, the fighter should be moving in and out of range, picking his opponent off. See figs 54 to 55 (previous page).

Pad work is the nearest thing you can get to sparring and can be very enjoyable to the fighter, and the pad-man.

Shadow Sparring

Shadow Sparring, is as the name suggests, working with your partner in the ring attacking as your partner defends and defending as your partner attacks.

The obvious difference from full blown sparring being that the punches Don't make contact. You should be just out of range as you throw your punches, paying attention to what your partner is doing and trying to counter attack him.

Because the punches are not landing, it is important that your partner co-operates with you as you attack and defend.

CHAPTER TEN
Counter Attacking

Counter attacking is a very effective way of scoring points on your opponent. To mount your own attack, you must first, either find or create an opening in your opponent's defence. In counter attacking, on the other hand, more times than not, as your opponent starts to attack, he will probably leave himself open to a counter attack. The hard bit from your point of view, is having the confidence to stand your ground as your opponent throws his punches and then throw your own at the same time.

Countering the Jab with a Jab

The easiest punch to counter, as you might guess, is the jab.

Fig. 57.

The Art of Boxing

You already know the first step of the counter, that is to parry the punch as before. Now as you parry the punch, step forward with your left foot and throw your own jab. See fig 57 (previous page).

As with all counter punches, the whole process is one movement, as your opponent throws his punch, you should start to throw yours, this will catch your opponent in a vulnerable position and also break his rhythm and spoil his attack.

Countering a Right Hand with a Right Hand

To counter attack a right hand, the same principal applies. As your opponent throws the right hand, parry the punch and at the same time step forward with your left foot and throw your own right hand. This is a very effective punch as you can see, your opponent is coming on to your right hand as he throws his own. See fig 58.

Fig. 58.

Practice these simple counter attacks with your partner. For safety sake, your partner should throw the punch wearing a glove, and take the counter punch on a pad, which you can hit with full force. As you become

Counter Attacking

more relaxed with the move, you will start to see more openings, such as a right hand counter, followed by a left hook. Don't forget your footwork, remember, as you go forward with the attack, keep stepping in as your opponent goes back.

You can start to put combination attacks together in light sparring situations working off your opponent, who will be throwing lots of punches for you to counter. It is worth noting, your opponent should be well protected with a head guard and body and groin protectors.

In chapter five, we looked at defence. Slipping inside and outside as our opponent threw his punches. Now we can move one step further and look at countering from these positions.

Countering a Right Hand with a Left Uppercut to the Body

As your opponent throws his right hand, step to the left, with your left foot, at the same time bend your left knee and turn your right shoulder toward your opponent.

Fig. 59.

As the punch is thrown, you can see how open your opponent is to a left hand counter, either to the body or head. See fig 59.

73

The Art of Boxing

From this position, turn your left hand palm facing in. Now with your left elbow tight against your body, spin around to the right and at the same time, throw the left hand to the body. The punch should be thrown at about 45 degrees to your body, landing under your opponents ribs.

Don't forget to use your hips to create the power behind the punch. As you will see with practice, close range punching, requires a lot of leverage from the hips and legs.

Fig. 60.

Countering a Right Hand with a Left Uppercut to the Head

Slipping outside your opponent's right hand, turn your left hand palm facing inward. This time throw the punch to the head, the punch should be thrown straight up, elbow tucked in, connecting underneath your opponents chin. Punch through with your hips as before. See fig 60.

Counter Attacking

Countering a Jab with a Right Hand to the Body

The same counter is used for the jab. Keep your feet still and bend to the right at the same time bending your knees. Turn your left shoulder towards your opponent. Turn your palm inwards and throw the right hand into your opponents body, keeping your elbow tight to your body. See fig 61.

Fig. 61.

Countering a Jab with a Right Uppercut to the Head

The same applies for the uppercut to the head, bend to the right at the same time bend your knees. Turn your hand palm facing inwards. The punch should land underneath the chin.

Fig. 62.

The Art of Boxing

Again, it is important to use your hips to create the power. As you start to throw the punch concentrate on spinning your hips, and thrusting upwards at the same time. Because your opponent has come forward and you have slipped inside or outside, there is no need for any long arm extension, keep the whole movement tight and powerful. See fig 62 (previous page).

As you continue to practice, you will see that you can throw almost any punch in a counter attack, however it should be noted that your counter attack can also be counter attacked. Confused? Well, if you think about it, we have already looked at drawing your opponent out by feigning a punch, thus making him throw a punch. So if your opponent feigns a punch and you 'Go for it', you will start to counter attack a punch that was never thrown, and your opponent will then counter attack your attack.

I hope this chapter isn't confusing you too much. You should now be starting to appreciate how complicated a fight can be. It's not just a case of throwing punches, as most people think, there is a great deal to think about when you are in the thick of battle.

Fig. 63.

Countering a Right with a Right Uppercut

As your opponent throws the right hand, parry the punch with your left hand and counter with a right upper cut to the chin. Keep your elbow tucked into your side, and spin your hips to the left. You won't need to step in, because your opponent will be coming forward onto your punch. See fig 63 (previous page).

Countering a Right Hand with a Right Hand to the Body

As your opponent throws the right hand, step forwards with your left foot, and throw a straight right to your opponent's body. As you can see from the position of the fighter's left foot. You need to take a long step, lowering your own body. Notice how square the hips are. This shows the total commitment to the punch, with the right shoulder following through. See fig 64.

Fig. 64.

The Art of Boxing

CHAPTER ELEVEN
Fitness

Safety

If you are entering the world of fitness for the first time, or returning after a rest, it might be worth getting the once over from your GP. Obviously if you are over weight or very unfit, take extra care as you go through the book, there is no need to rush. The important thing to remember, is that you are on a learning curve, and as such you should go at your own pace.

One of the hardest things an athlete has to deal with, is injury or illness. I have lost count of the amount of times I have watched people strapping sprained or bruised joints before a training session. Although this dedication to training is admirable, it is also foolhardy and leaves the athlete open to long term injury.

Don't be afraid to take a day off if you are feeling under the weather, training while not one hundred percent can leave you feeling worse than when you started. But don't use imaginary sniffs or coughs to skip training either, as I will say many times as we go through the book, it's you who will be taking the punches.

Warming Up

Before any kind of exercise, you must always warm up. That is, stretch and loosen your muscles ready for the strenuous workout ahead. To do

The Art of Boxing

this you must first start with the large muscle groups, and increase the pace getting warmer and warmer, until you are ready for the workout. These exercises will also help you to stay flexible and supple.

Defining Fitness

It is difficult to define fitness. The kind of fitness needed by a footballer is completely different from that of a marathon runner. Boxers are considered by many people to be amongst the fittest athletes of all. The reason for this, is because the boxer needs the stamina of the long distance runner together with the short explosive bursts of a footballer. Couple to these, the footwork of a dancer and the strength of a gymnast, and you will start to see what I mean. As you become fitter, you will need to separate your training into two sessions - Technical training and Fitness training. The reason for this is because the type of fitness training needed by a boxer is varied and extremely hard. So to do your technical training justice, you should be fresh when you begin.

The main features a boxer needs from his training are Flexibility, Stamina, Strength and Speed. Generally speaking, boxers don't do a lot of training with heavy weights, unless they need to retain or put weight on. The majority of a boxer's strength comes from circuit training, which we will look at later.

Stamina

The main form of stamina training, takes the form of running. I have always enjoyed running, but I appreciate it isn't everyone's cup of tea. If you prefer to ride a bike, that's fine. The distance you need to cover depends on your age and how overweight you are, if at all. If you are running, three miles would be the minimum distance you need. And if you are riding a bike, ten miles. And don't forget you can coast down hill on a bike, so choose a flat route. Just make sure you put the miles in every week. You will also increase your level of fitness, simply by doing your normal bag work, which is an excellent aerobic workout.

Recently, boxercise has become very popular as a way of keeping fit, and although it is not considered real boxing training, it is a good testimony to how highly boxing training is regarded as a form of keep fit.

Technical Work Out

The majority of your training session, will be done in rounds. Starting with two minute rounds and one minute's rest and working up to three minutes and one minutes rest.

A typical session should consist of four rounds of skipping, four rounds of shadow boxing and four rounds of bag work. Apart from these, you should spend time working on set piece movements in front of the mirror such as combinations and footwork.

Circuit Training

Circuit Training is an integral part of boxing, and you should always end your session with at least one kind of circuit. One of my favourites, is a Ton-Up. Ten exercises with ten repetitions of each one. This circuit is a good all round workout incorporating ,legs, arms, chest, back and shoulders, as well as abdomen, although the abdomen should be exercised separately as should the neck. **See chart 1.**

The Art of Boxing

Chart 1

**Press Ups
Sit Ups
Burpee Jumps
Bounce Press-Ups
Jack-Knife Sit Ups
Star Jumps
Close Hand Press-Ups
Bent Knee Sit-Ups
Squat Jumps
Wide Arm Press-Ups**

Press-ups

Start with your hands shoulder width apart, directly under your chest.

1.

2.

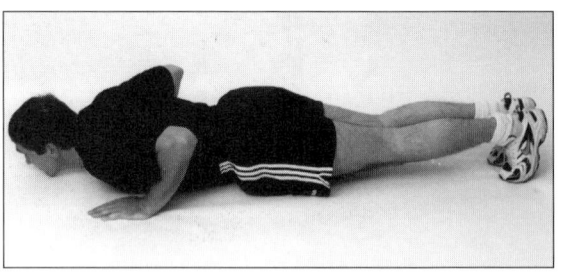

Lower yourself until your chest is just off the floor, making sure you are looking forwards throughout the exercise, and keeping your back straight. Then return to the start position.

It's important to keep your elbows tucked into your sides, this will help isolate your biceps and triceps.

3.

Sit-ups

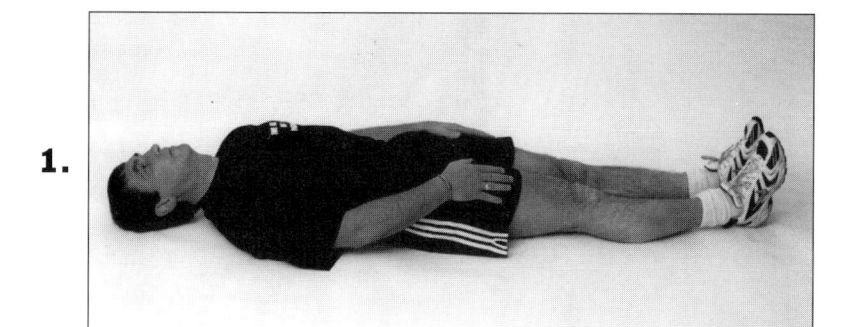

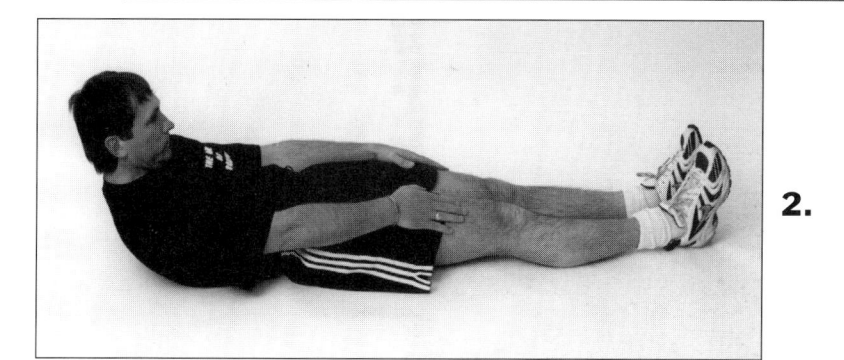

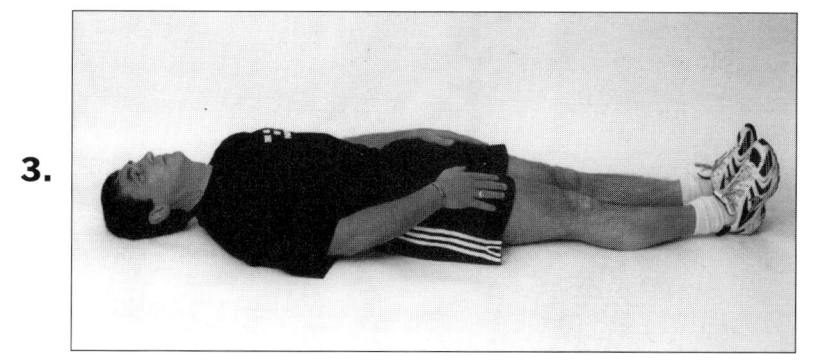

1.

2.

3.

Start by laying flat on the floor with your legs straight and your hands placed on your thighs. Lifting your head and then your shoulders off the floor, slide your hands along your thighs until your finger tips touch your knees. It's important to use a rolling motion in order to protect and isolate your lower back.

The Art of Boxing

Burpee jumps

1.
2. & 4.
3.
5.
6.

Start in a standing position. Bend your knees to a squat and then throw your feet back to form a press-up position. Return to the squat position and then jump straight up, landing back in a squat position. You will need to find your feet with this exercise, as you can see it is quite complicated, but with practise, the whole exercise will start to flow.

Fitness

Bounce press-ups

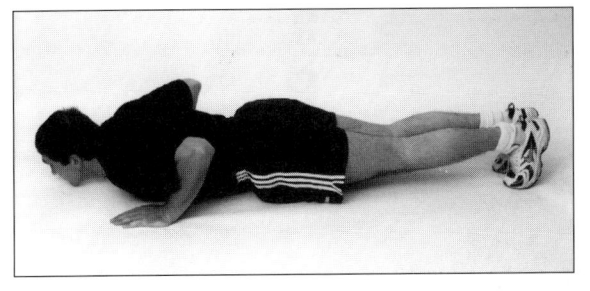

1.

2.

Start in the normal press-up position, but now as you lower your body bounce back up and try to clap your hands together before landing and repeating the exercise.

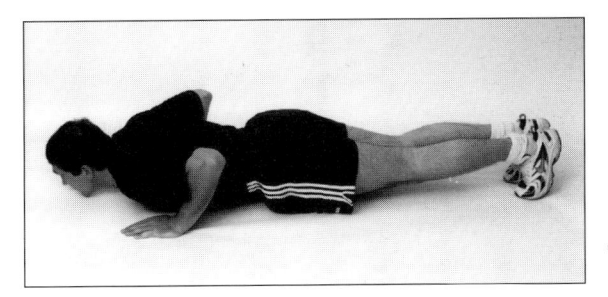

3.

4.

This one is a little more difficult both to execute and to photograph as you can see.

The Art of Boxing

Jack-knife sit-ups

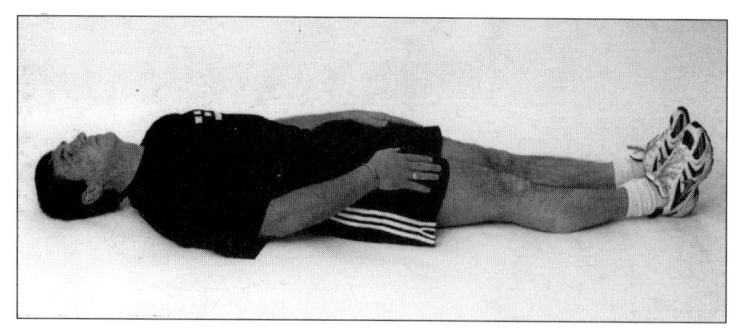

1.

2.

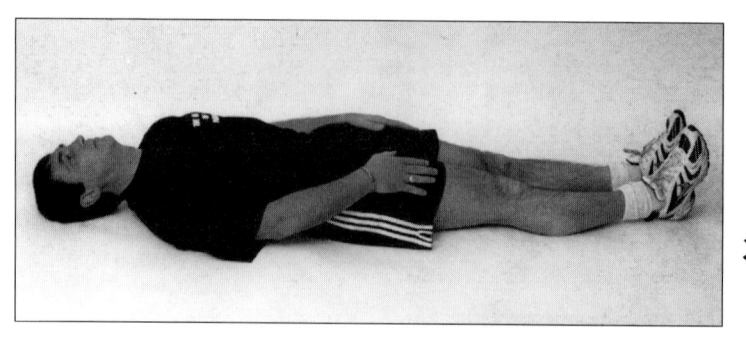

3.

Start in the normal sit-up position. Then raise your legs so that you touch your feet as you sit up. Make sure you keep your back and legs straight throughout the exercise. Again, this exercise takes some practise, so be patient and the timing will come. Be careful not to allow your feet to land too heavily during the exercise.

Fitness

Star jumps

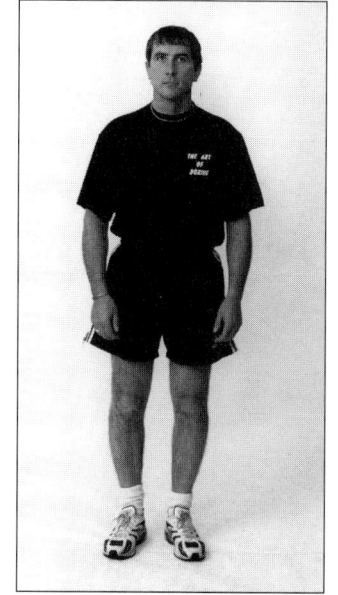

1.

2.

3.

4.

Start in a standing position. Bend you knees to a squat and then jump up and reach out to make the 'star' shape. As you land return to the squat position and repeat the exercise.

Close hand press-ups

1.

Start in the press-up position, but this time bring your hands together so that your thumbs and fore-fingers touch. Now perform the basic press-up exercise.

2.

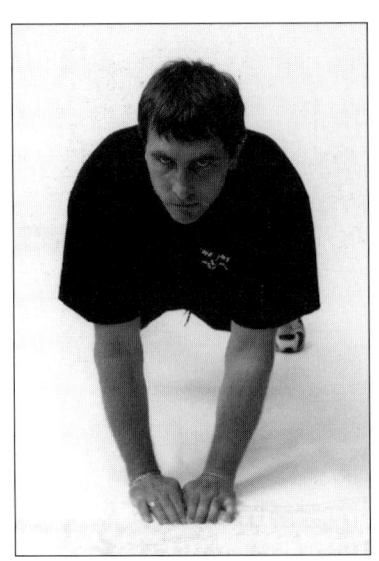

This type of press-up isolates your triceps and is a good upper body workout.

3.

Bent knee sit-ups

1.

2.

3.

Start in a lying position with your knees bent. Sit up and bring your chest to your knees. As before, the hands are kept by your sides, and remember to roll your torso, head and shoulders first.

The Art of Boxing

Squat jumps

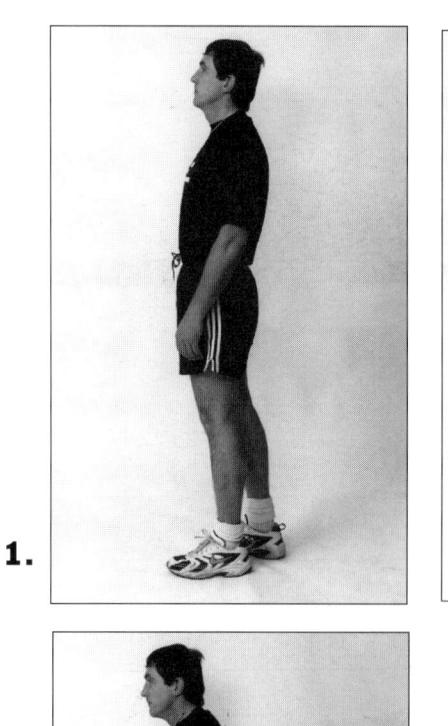

1.

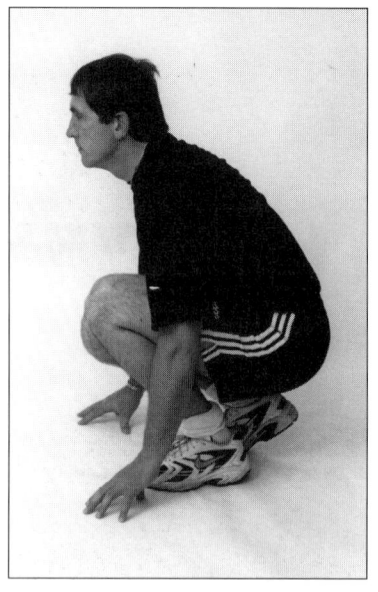

2.

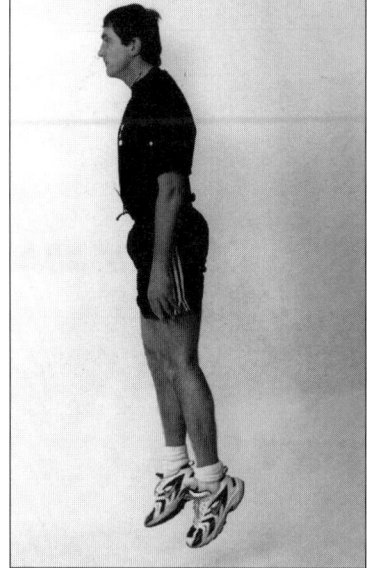

3.

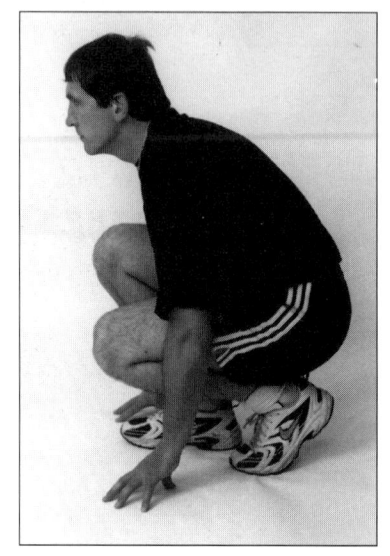

4.

From a standing position, drop to a squat with one foot slightly forward of the other. Jump straight up and return to the squat position but this time with the other foot forward.

Fitness

Wide arm press-ups

1.

2.

3.

Start in the press-up position but this time with your hands as far apart as possible, at least twice shoulder width. You may point your fingers to the side or forward. Then perform the press-up exercise using your back muscles. Done properly, you should feel your upper back muscles working to full effect.

This type of circuit is not timed and normally takes between 2 and 3 minutes. Remember, it is not a race, the emphasis should be on quality.

Chart 2 shows a timed circuit using 6 exercises. The main difference between this type and the ton-up is that you are required to do as many repetitions as you can at each station in the time allotted. Although the quality of the exercise will reduce slightly, your stamina will improve with the increase in intensity. The circuit is either a 2 or 3 minute work-out, with each station being of 20 or 30 second duration. Unlike the ton-up, this circuit requires your complete focus and is intended to represent a heavy round of boxing.

Chart 2

Sit-ups
Press-ups (feet on a chair)
Step-ups (on to chair)
Bent knee jack knife sit-ups
Close hand press-ups
Burpee jumps

Abdominal

When exercising the abdominal muscles, lay on your back and try not to use your back muscles. There are lots of different kinds of exercises for the abdomen, try a few that you feel comfortable with and don't be afraid to experiment.

Neck

The neck muscles are also very important to the boxer. A strong set of neck muscles will absorb a punch. The 'wrestlers bridge' is one of the best exercises to strengthen the neck.

Lay on your back with your feet pulled up underneath your thighs. Now push your bodyweight up and over using your arms, whilst at the same time, pulling your head underneath your shoulders. Be very careful at first, you can take some of your bodyweight on your hands until you have strengthened your neck. Once you feel comfortable with this exercise you can start to slowly rock backwards and forwards onto the top of your forehead. This is a difficult exercise to master, so be careful and you will reap the rewards. (If in doubt - look at Evander Holyfield!)

Like most sports, fitness training is only a part of the build up to the actual event. But without a high level of competitive fitness you are going to find yourself in serious trouble. However, that doesn't mean you can't enjoy your fitness training, which is why training to music has always been helpful to boxers. In the early part of this century, boxers used to skip in time to popular jazz tunes of the day. Training with music helps with timing as well as rhythm, and also helps take your mind off the hard work. Don't forget to enjoy your fitness training.

CHAPTER TWELVE
Sparring

So finally we come to full blown sparring. Hopefully you will have gained enough knowledge reading through this book to enable you to hold your own in the ring.

However, reading a book is one thing but actually getting in the ring and doing the business is another. Which is why this chapter, although one of the smallest, is probably one of the most important.

Light Sparring

As I have already said, sparring is the only way you can actually find out if your punches work. So you can now begin to spar with your partner, putting into practice everything you have learned.

As with punching, sparring will also tell you if your defence works. Unfortunately if it doesn't, you are in for a painful time. Don't get too frustrated if you are getting caught with a lot of punches to start with, you will soon start to loosen up and relax.

The whole point of light sparring is to get you used to the idea of throwing punches at a moving target and at the same time defend and counter punches coming the other way. Work with your sparring partner and don't be afraid to experiment.

Heavy Sparring

In time you will become cool and confident in the ring which is a wonderful feeling and one very few people actually experience. However, there is still one lesson you need to undertake. That is, to be pressure tested. You will never know how you operate under pressure if you are not actually pressured in the ring.

Honesty is the only policy here. So find at least two good quality boxers and get them to push you to the limit. The idea is not to knock you out but to continually pressurise you with hard punches, making you literally work to survive.

Once you have come through one or two hard sparring sessions, take time to reflect on how you fared. It's only after these hard sessions that chinks start to appear in your armour. So be honest with yourself and analyse your weak points as well as your strong points and start working on them. But don't be too hard on yourself, no one's perfect!

There is no need to use heavy sparring all of the time, light sparring is perfectly good enough to put the theory into practice. You can step up the intensity if you think you are getting a bit lazy or one or two bad habits are creeping in.

CHAPTER THIRTEEN
Why Boxing?

A strange question you might think. Well yes, perhaps it is a bit odd considering we are at the end of the book. But did you actually sit down and think why you wanted to learn how to box? Let's face it, boxing hurts, which is why I have decided to write this chapter last.

Over the years I have tried my hand, and foot, at most of the martial arts including Karate, Kung-Fu, Aikido, Judo, Thai Boxing and Tae-Kwon-Do, to name but a few. All in all, I enjoyed myself and met some wonderful people along the way.

I have been asked on many occasions, what I thought of the martial arts. My response was, and always will be that I have got the utmost respect for anyone who is prepared to stand up and 'Do the business' in front of an audience. Although there are different opinions on what doing the business actually means, my opinion is that boxing is one of the most honest forms of combat I have ever come across. Not in the sense of hitting below the belt, but in the sense of one on one, best man wins.

The Art of Boxing

Unlike the majority of martial arts, there are no belts to say how good you are. The only thing that will testify to that, is your last fight.

Don't get me wrong, I have had the great pleasure of meeting one or two superb fighters from the karate world. But with the exception of Thai boxing and the grappling arts, I have to say that I have still to find anything to equal the ferocity of boxing.

For this reason boxing is also potentially one of the most dangerous fighting forms. As you will know from your heavy sparring sessions, once you are in the ring and the bell goes, there is nowhere to run.

So to repeat my first question, why boxing? Why put yourself in the position of being beaten about the head for no reason. Why risk the humiliation of being knocked out in front of your friends and family? Why fight when every natural instinct is telling you to run?

I'm sure we have all heard the local expert saying he would take Holyfield on for a couple of million and just keep running. Now that you have gained a better insight into boxing, you will appreciate just how silly that statement is.

The vast majority of people don't understand how much damage a punch from a professional boxer could do to the average man on the street.

So how do boxers manage to take punches from their opponents round after round with out any side effects. Fitness plays a large part. I have said many times in the book, a fit strong boxer will always overcome a weaker opponent.

Why Boxing?

The real reason however, is a bit more complicated. You will know by now that no mater how much you try, you can not exercise your chin, which is what take's most of the punishment.

To understand the real warrior, you have to pull back the hard outer layers and look to the inside. This is where you will find the heart of the boxer and more to the point, the sole. This is where the fighter finds the strength to ignore every natural and understandable instinct that is telling him not to get into the ring, but to stay at home where it is safe.

This is where every fight is won and lost, not in the ring, but deep down in the boxers sole. This is where the fight begins, not against an opponent but against yourself. If you can win this fight then you can win the easy bit in the ring. If however, you cannot win this one, no amount of training will help you to win in the ring.

Looking at boxing from nature's point of view, there is absolutely nothing normal about boxing. We have spent the last 300,000 years doing our best to avoid conflict, unless it was absolutely necessary, so why stand toe to toe with someone and fight, when there is no need.

A good point, looking at it from that point of view. But looking at it from the point of view that nature will only tolerate the survival of the fittest, then there is a lot of point.

Of course a lot of people would say, there is no need for that kind of mentality in today's society and perhaps they are right. I could say the same thing about horse racing. What is the point of racing a dumb animal around a field when there is nothing to escape from.

The Art of Boxing

So what makes a good fighter, and more to the point how do you win the fight that is constantly going on deep down in your sole. This is a very personal fight, one which takes place out of the gaze of the public, one which cannot be cheated nor avoided.

Unfortunately many boxers refuse to acknowledge the natural fear within themselves. They seem to think it is a sign of weakness, so they block it out, pretending it is not there.

This is OK until the fight is at its thickest and you have got nothing left. The punches are landing thick and fast, the pounding echoes in your ears, punch after punch thumping off your head. Your head feels like it is about to explode, you try to respond but nothing happens. It's now that the voice from within starts to talk to you, saying you should lie down and take the count, "he is to good for you", "why take all of those punches when you can just lie down and it will be all over?"

There is a common misconception about fear. A lot of boxers confuse fear with other emotions, as the fight draws near they start to have self doubt. The mind will do anything it can to stop you from getting into the ring. What a lot of boxers don't realise, is that their opponent is feeling exactly the same thing. Nature can see no point in the fight so it tries everything it can to stop us from doing it.

The hard bit is to override this natural feeling and take control of our own thoughts. We all know the saying, mind over matter, but just how much thought have you ever given to it. It is true to say that he who controls his own mind controls his own destiny.

Why Boxing?

There are lots of stories from the martial arts world about old masters who could walk on burning embers, or focus all of their inner energy and punch a whole through a man with a bare fist. We can all recall similar stories, the point of the matter is that the feats were not that hard physically but mentally almost impossible.

So where does that leave the poor old boxer? Well up until recently, pretty much on his own. Although boxing has become one of the most specialised forms of unarmed combat, it has neglected the inner fight along the way, and as we know this is by far the most important fight of all.

Because of the uniqueness of boxing, the people who participate are also unique and are often thought of as almost mystical. For this reason we tend to look upon these modern gladiators with awe, perhaps this is because of the incredible bravery they show as they step into the ring leaving the safety and comfort of everyday life behind.

Perhaps its because as we sit in our own comfortable world and watch them on television, we are secretly stepping into the ring to take on the fearsome warrior in the opposite corner. What must it be like to have to face such an awesome foe in front of thousands of people? Of course most of us will never feel the incredible fear as we climb the steps to the ring or the thumping beat of your heart as it pumps adrenaline around your body, or the horrible feeling of loneliness as the bell sounds its first toll.

In the sanitised push button high tech world of today, it is the boxer who stands out alone, as did the great warriors of old. We will never know

The Art of Boxing

what it is like to stand on the edge and look into the eyes of the unknown. We will never be able to feel the incredible joy of a battle won and the adulation that is reserved for the greatest victors of all. This is why boxers will always be kings in the sporting world and heroes in ours.

The Art of Boxing

JA-Tech Studios Ltd
Publications Department
178a Grange Road
Longford
Coventry
West Midlands CV6 6DA
Tel / Fax: (024) 76 36 4444 - 24 Hour Hotline
e-mail: jatech@the-studios.freeserve.co.uk

With over 40 years combined Martial Arts experience, Jim Burns and Al Peasland have joined forces to produce some of the most comprehensive instructional publications on Self Protection and Competitive Combat.

For over 25 years Jim Burns has been involved in Martial Arts, specialising in Western Boxing and Muay Thai Boxing. Jim is also an experienced Nightclub Doorman in Coventry and a qualified Professional Bodyguard. Because of this Jim has the advantage of having tested his skills in both the sports and pavement arenas. His many qualifications include:- BBC Professional Trainer, BTBC 10th Khan Muay Thai, BTBC Qualified Coach, BTBC Qualified Referee & Judge, BCA Instructor.

Jim Burns

Having 12 years Martial Arts experience incorporating Karate, Boxing and Wrestling, Alan is recognised as Geoff Thompson's Senior Instructor. Alan is also a qualified Professional Bodyguard and an experienced Nightclub Doorman. His qualifications include:-

ABA Boxing Coach, JKA 1st Dan Shotokan, EKGB 3rd Dan Shotokan, BCA 3rd Dan Instructor, 1st Dan Sambo Wrestling, BAWA Freestyle Wrestling Coach, BAWA Greco Roman Wrestling Coach.

Alan Peasland

The Art of Boxing

JA-Tech Studios Ltd
Publications Department
178a Grange Road
Longford
Coventry
West Midlands CV6 6DA
Tel / Fax (024) 76 36 4444 - 24 Hour Hotline
e-mail: jatech@the-studios.freeserve.co.uk

Latest Video Releases

For More Information
Call our 24 Hour Hotline
All Major Credit Cards Accepted

Tel: (024) 76 36 4444

e-mail: jatech@the-studios.freeserve.co.uk

Now that you've read the book, why not compliment this with some superb live action footage from Pro trainer Jim Burns.

Volume 1

Starts with the basics providing an educational and enjoyable look at basic stance and punching techniques.

Volumes 2 & 3

Continue through the more advanced techniques leading onto intricate combinations and culminating in some fast and furious sparring.

Jim is helped by Top Boxing Coach Al Peasland, and some experienced fighters including big punching heavyweight Andy Burns and top Karate International Ian McCranor.

The Art of Boxing

The most complete book on the subject of Close Protection. 330 pages, over 100 photographs and numerous illustrations. Every subject explained in detail by one of the world's most experienced bodyguards.

'The Modern Bodyguard'
by Peter Consterdine
£27.49
(inc. UK p & p)

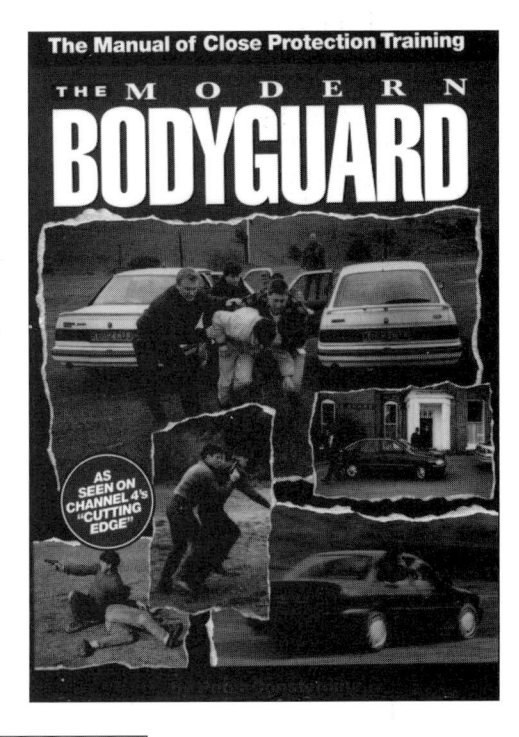

This manual is not another 'martial arts in jeans' type of self defence book. It combines detailed concepts from the world of bodyguarding, with the very best of self defence.

'Streetwise'
by Peter Consterdine
£27.49
(inc. UK p & p)

The Art of Boxing

The manual of Intense training for Combat

FIT TO FIGHT

Be Fit to fight, develop that mental edge

BY PETER CONSTERDINE

Peter is acknowledged as one of Britain's fittest martial artists. A book not only for the martial artist, but for anyone who wants to be truly fit.

'Fit To Fight'
by Peter Consterdine
£17.49
(inc. UK p & p)

To order any of these products or for a FREE colour catalogue, containing the full range of books and videos from
Protection Publications
please call our 24hr hotline
Telephone
0113 2429686
Major credit cards accepted.

FROM FITNESS TO SURVIVAL ON THE STREETS.
The complete collection from Protection Publications

books & videos

Protection PUBLICATIONS

Visit out website on:

www.protection-publications.co.uk